RAYS

New York, 1925

Pir-o-Murshid Inayat Khan

RAYS

by
Kismet Dorothea Stam

EAST-WEST PUBLICATIONS FONDS B.V.
THE HAGUE

This book was written in Suresnes (France) in 1927

East-West Publications Fonds b.v.

P.O. Box 7617, The Hague, Holland

No part of this book may be reproduced in any form, by print, photoprint, microfilm or any other means, without written permission from the publisher.

ISBN 90 70104 22 9

Contents

Foreword	7
Part I	11
Part II	21
Part III	57
Part IV	73
Glossary	147

The following pages contain some few incidents from the life of the Blessed One, and some of his words from the time when he lived in human guise among us.

Foreword

This book has been written by one of the close collaborators of the great Sufi master, Pir-o-Murshid Hazrat Inayat Khan, who brought the Sufi Message to the Western world in the years 1910-1926. In these memoires the accent is not so much on the historical sequence of events, but rather on the atmosphere of the great teacher and how he spoke and behaved in various life-circumstances.

The book was written shortly after the death of Murshid Inayat Khan and not a word has been changed so that the original style is preserved. The book radiates reverence and should be read as a book of meditation.

The publisher

8

Why did the fragrance of the flowers outflow
If not to breathe with benediction sweet
Across His path? Why did the soft wind blow
If not to kiss the ground before His feet?

Ghalib.

PART I

When Murshid[1] was a little boy, His father wanted Him to practise, playing and singing during the night. As His mother was so much against this, His father asked: 'But if He does not practise, then what will He be when He is grown up?' 'You will see', His mother answered, 'you will see'.

(Note: told by Murshid.)

There is a custom in India that when an aged person forefeels that this veil of mortality will be lifted from his soul, he calls those whom he loves, and gives them his blessing:

It happened at the time when Murshid was quite a young boy that one day He sang the songs His grandfather had taught Him, before the members of the household. He sang so beautifully that the old ladies of the family were strongly reminded of that which is beyond the screen of this mortal existence. They were moved to tears. They called the boy, and holding their hands over His head, they blessed Him.

The primal appeal of that Voice which one day would conquer the world.

(Note: told by Murshid.)

As a child Murshid used to hear the friends of Moula Bakhsh[2] sing the Sufi-songs about the heavenly wine which brings to those who drink it divine intoxication.

One day Murshid heard a servant apply the words 'sour wine' to the contents of a jug in the storeroom of Moula Bakhsh House. The servant meant 'vinegar'. But the boy only paid attention to the sound of 'wine', he did not mind the attribute. And in His eager longing to experience that of which the singers had sung, He one day went secretly to this jug and courageously drank from the acid draught, with the hope and conviction that one day the divine intoxication would manifest to Him.

(Note: told by Murshid.)

Inayat once asked His father: 'Shall I be a Nabi[3], father?'

His father was very much frightened and said: 'Never say such a thing again!'

(Note: told by Murshid.)

As a young musician Murshid once went in a Hindu-temple to worship the One Who is the God of all. When Murshid came out, He greeted the guardian at the temple-door, addressing him as 'brother'. The Hindu, on hearing a Moslim say 'brother' to him, became so furious that Murshid afterwards said: 'He was ready to kill me.' Seeing his anger Murshid humbly bowed before the man and said: 'Excuse me, sir, I forget; I am your servant.'

(Note: told by Murshid.)

When Murshid and His brothers came to the United States for the first time, their rhythm was the rhythm of India, the land where the idea of time plays little or no part, where everyone lives in eternity. They were accustomed to do as every Indian musician does before he begins to play: he tunes his instrument for a long time, and by doing so he tunes his own soul and the souls of those who listen.

Murshid and the brothers once accepted an engagement to play and sing in a place where many other performances were given before and after it was their turn to appear before the public. When that moment was approaching, they quietly began with the tuning of their instruments. How great was their astonishment when the tuning was finished: the whole performance was over.

(Note: told by Murshid.)

20

PART II

When Murshid lived in London during the time of the war, a detective visited the house where Murshid was staying. Knowing himself to be an official, he felt to have the right to investigate every corner of it as if he himself were the owner of it all. With a proprietor's air he opened the door of the room where Murshid was present. Then, beholding Murshid who was sitting in deep meditation, he did not enter the room. But his soul entered that kingdom which is not of the earth.

And he became a mureed.[4]

As it has been said in the Scriptures: 'One glimpse of Thy glorious vision maketh me eternal.'

Murshid was once asked how one could best control undesirable influences.

Murshid said: 'By not acknowledging them.'

Many mureeds have criticized Murshid's choice of making Suresnes the centre of the Summer School activities.

Murshid said: 'It was destined.'Suresnes' in Sanscrit, means 'the Lord himself', and 'Val d'Or' can be interpreted as: the place where the Vali, the Master, moves around.'

Murshid said: 'Suresnes will be another Meccah.'

When in the garden of Fazal Manzil[5] an address for Viladat Day[6] was presented to the mureeds in order to be signed by them, someone said in jest: 'Can I read it, that I may be sure I am not signing my death-decree?'

The mureed who presented the address, readily answered: 'Rather know that it is your 'life'-decree.'

There was a mureed who was
digging within himself, and who for
being was dealing with some mud. He ԭ
drowned in despair. He went to anothe.
mureed and said: 'it is only because we are the
worst sinners that Murshid has come to
stretch to us His helping hand.'

The other mureed had come to the
realization of the life-giving truth of the
words: 'When Thou art before me I rise upon
wings, and my burden becometh light; but
when my little self riseth before mine eyes I
drop to the earth, and all its weight falleth
upon me.'

He joyfully said: 'I would gladly be
worser than the worst sinner if that could have
brought me to Murshid's Feet.'

In the summer of the fourtieth year Murshid one day asked the children what they would later on do with Abba's[7] photograph. One of them said: 'I shall give it the most beautifull place in my room.' The other said: 'I shall always put it near me on the table.' The third said: 'I shall hang it on the wall in such a way that when I open my eyes in the morning I shall first of all see Abba's picture.' Mamuli said in her broken baby's language: 'I shall put it on the roof of my house.'

Murshid wished yellow tiles to be incrusted in a certain chimney at Fazal Manzil. The man who was concerned with it, was requested to bring them out. He was astonished. 'Yellow tiles?' he said, 'they don't exist.' Murshid made the man come in His presence. Murshid said: 'You see, such yellow tiles ......'. 'Yes yes,' the man immediately replied, 'I'll find them, Sir!'

A few days later the yellow tiles were there.

Murshid once told a story about His boys: that during the time of the summer school Murshid one day found Bhaijan[9] in a very thoughtful attitude in the garden of Fazal Manzil. Murshid asked him about what he was planning, and the answer was: 'I want to give a lecture.' 'At the dinnertable', Murshid suggested. 'No', was the reply, 'in the big hall, before all the mureeds.' 'You arrange it,' Murshid said, smiling.

Some moments afterwards a mureed happened to pass where Bhaijan was standing. She felt inclined to ask about what he was thinking so deeply. 'About a lecture I want to give before the mureeds,' he said. So she arranged it for him, and in the corner-house several mureeds came together to listen. First he kept a long silence and then he spoke on the subject of 'love and patience'. He was nine years old then. He spoke with great enthusiasm; and he gave as an example for what he had to say an instance from the play 'The Bogeyman' which had just been given some days before. 'Look at the lover', he said; 'there he takes a poison and kills himself, whereas, if he had had the patience to pursue the one he loved, -how different life would have become for him.' And so he continued.

After some days Bhaiyajan[10] also expressed the wish to give a lecture. He saw his elder brother having such a success, and he had perhaps just caught the sense of the word 'inspiration'. So he also wanted to experience it. Everything was arranged for him. Many mureeds came together and were seated in rows before the speaker's chair. He solemnly took his place in front of them, seriously uttered: 'Silence', and closed his eyes. After some five minutes, here and there a curious mureed ventured a stealthy glance to see whether something was happening. But nothing happened. Bhaiyajan was there, his eyes tight closed. When a considerable time had passed some inquisitive mureed asked: 'Bhaiyajan?' Bhaiyajan slowly opened his eyes. 'Your lecture, Bhaiyajan', the mureed said.

The answer was: 'It has not yet come'.

Murshid often smiled at the character of the people of a certain country, a character which can best be described by a little story Murshid told.

A mureed was waiting on the platform of a railway-station, his hands full of things he did not want to entrust to any porter, with before him on the ground a small box with fragile contents. As the train was rushing in, he called a porter and said: 'Please take that box, but handle it most carefully.' The man indifferently looked another side, whistling a little tune. The mureed knew that this train only stopped for a few minutes, so he got a desperate feeling of helplessness. Then he had a psychological inspiration, and he said: 'Man, please take that box; drop it, break it, or destroy it!'

Immediately the porter most carefully lifted the box, carried it to a well-chosen compartment, and softly deposited it there.

Before the Oriental room[11] a mureed was waiting his turn of having an interview with Murshid. He was a learned man, a doctor, who prematurely had realised the futility of all things, and consequently got into raging moods about the things existing.

'Love, harmony and beauty!' he said, 'He lectures about love, harmony and beauty! And what, if I shot a bullet through my head in the midst of such a lecture, so that..........' Here he used some very crude and realistic terms to describe the resulting occurrences, and continued: 'Would He still speak of love, harmony and beauty; would all these sheep-like people continue to believe in it?!'

At this culmination-point of his rage, the time for his interview had arrived; so, with a furious air, he entered Murshid's room.

After the seven minutes had passed he came out, radiating. The front-door was opened to him, and a breath of the early summer-breeze filled the corridor.

Then he used an expression in his own language: 'What a blessing', he said, 'that it is such 'godly' weather to-day!'

A lady with horticultural tendencies, after reading Murshid's article about 'Woman's place in the East and West,' asked:

'What part may Eastern woman play in gardening?'

Murshid said: 'She may pick the flowers.'

Seeing how generally Western woman finds her joy and forgets her sorrow in a never ceasing activity, and thereby loses her opportunity of realising that which is beyond the realm of action, Murshid once said: 'Indian women can do nothing, can fool their time.'

Murshid once said after a strenuous day when still there was work to be done: 'It is better never to leave anything unfinished.'

'How amazing!' a mureed said, 'in this pioneer's life full of struggles and difficulties there is no end to my enthusiasm and strength, whereas formerly I felt so soon exhausted'.

Murshid said: 'Now you can forget yourself.'

His graciousness balancing their barren blindness.

As it has been said: 'He loves them! But: 'they love Him?'

When one of the workers once showed an inclination for foreign literature, Murshid said: 'There is the Message[12]. A whole life-time is not sufficient to give it.'

'I have been thinking and thinking,' a mureed said, 'about what is meant by 'the Message.' And as a conclusion I find that the Message is a vibration, a vibration which has to be brought to the world at large, to tune it to a certain pitch.'

Said another mureed: 'Murshid, it seemed to be so simple. I thought 'the Message' meant: 'Listen, O ye peoples of the earth, the Prophet has come!' But now I hear this mureed speak about the Message as being a vibration.'

Murshid said: 'His soul knows, but his mind troubles the vision of his soul.'

Someone said when taking up the work for the spreading of the Message: 'Murshid, I regret so much that my influence in my country is not greater. If only I had some influential aristocratic name.'

Murshid said: 'There is the aristocracy of the soul.'

One of the workers once came to Murshid, saying: 'It has all gone wrong, Murshid, it has all gone wrong'.

Murshid said: 'If you will adopt Murshid's way of working it will all come right'.

A mureed received a valuable present from someone whom he knew was not favourably inclined towards him, and had proved so in countless ways.

He asked: 'What shall I do? Shall I throw it away?'

Murshid said: 'Never! Each time when you look at it remember that even your enemies surrender to you.'

A mureed may listen with his heart's ears, he may apply the Prophet's words to all the garments of his soul; but rarely realizes he these words to be companions everlasting, who even whisper to his God-self.

Murshid said: 'In My service only you will be happy.'

There was a young, impatient mureed. He said: 'Ever since Murshid's words have reminded me of that Land of the soul, the longing for it has grown and grown. It seems as if for ages it has been growing!'

Murshid said: 'A certain amount of longing is needed.'

To Murshid one day there came a mureed whose mouth was full with the taste of endlessness. He asked: 'Shall ever I reach to the realization of the Light of Truth?'

Murshid said: 'Only trust in Murshid's love.'

There was a mureed who had no home. No house was his home, no country was his home. There was no place in the world which he could call his home.

Murshid said: 'Murshid's heart is your home.'

Many are the roads along which He has guided from attributes to essence, to each aspiring soul assigning what would illuminate his path.

There was one who craved for that which is beyond the fictive figures of the surface, beyond the shifting shadows of the depth. He uttered: 'Murshid, what shall I do?'

Murshid said: 'Nothing; wait.'

Murshid one day had to choose between Murshid's wish and a superhuman
effort. Seeing that Murshid was going to
choose the latter, a member of the family who
with all his heart wished that Murshid's way
should be smooth and easy, still wanted to
make the scale incline to the other side. He
said: 'Is it not pride?'

Murshid said: 'That is all one has.'

A mureed came to the realization of the vastness of that journey in which the life here on earth is like a drop compared to the sea.

He eagerly asked: 'Will this hand of Murshid guide me safely through the Maya[13] of life on the other side as it is guiding me through it here?'

Murshid said: 'Do you believe in the word of Rassoul[14]?'

A mureed asked: 'Why do the Moslims make an oath, saying: 'By the beard of the Prophet...'?

Murshid said: 'Every atom of the Prophet's Being is sacred.'

Murshid one day said: 'It cannot be told in words what it means to serve the Prophet.'

Murshid once answered the unspoken question of a mureed who was puzzled on seeing all the different paths human beings tread in order to reach the ultimate Goal.

Murshid said: 'There is but one direct way.'

A mureed eagerly asked: 'What could I do best to serve the Cause?'

Murshid said: 'I am the Cause.'

PART III

Standing before the panorama of New York's sky-scrapers Murshid said: 'Who has not seen New York, has not seen the world's greatest enthusiasm.'

When in the first act of Ansky's play 'The Dybbuck', the young student of the Kabbala[15] has died, the sage who appears on the scene utters the words: 'He saw beyond'.

Murshid said: 'These are the most beautiful words of the whole play.'

After the interviews during the afternoons in New York Murshid used to take a drive in 'Burrak',[16] as Murshid had baptised the motor-car of one of the mureeds. One day that mureed showed Murshid a church in Fifth Avenue, saying: 'This is the church where the fashionable people go.'

Since then Murshid always recognised this distinction by asking her on seeing a church-building: 'Is it a fashionable church?'

Murshid sometimes had the greatest fun about people's attitude.

In San Francisco there was a waiter who always became very confused while serving Murshid; very hurried, and red, and shaken. Perhaps Murshid's priestly outlook impressed him so much. Murshid used to address him as 'beta lăl', (my red son) which augmented his confusion.

One day Murshid said: 'Do you not wish to confess with me, beta lăl?'

'Another day, Sir', the man said, and got away as soon as he could.

It happened in a desert through which the Overland Limited passes before reaching its destination in the Far West, that it halted in one of those desert-towns with its peculiar atmosphere of aloofness from the world. When Murshid returned to the station at the end of the appointed stoppingtime, and reached the railway platform, the engine already had taken its start and was speedier and speedier moving its long trail of shifting waggons along their track.

Murshid did not pause for one moment, nor did He hasten what He Himself used to call His 'majestic walk'. There has been no shouting from others nor any outer sign of excitement. But the Limited has broken its journey and has stopped again until Murshid had safely entered.

Then it has re-begun its thousands miles' journey Westwards.

A mureed mentioned an enormous amount of wealth which would mean the fulfilment of a great wish Murshid fostered at the moment.

He said: 'May I offer it to you?'

Murshid said: 'No, thank you.'

In Los Angeles there was a little girl, about four years old, who could not take away her eyes from Murshid's face. All along her visit she gazed and gazed and was delighted when Murshid looked at her.

When the hour of parting came, her mother wanted to put on her little coat. But nothing could move her to allow anyone to do so. Neither her parents nor anyone present could induce her to be dressed for going. When they touched her, she made herself as stiff as a plank; and when they tried to manage these stiff little limbs, she became as slack as a harlequin.

Murshid took the little coat and said: 'First we put in one arm' The little girl smiled winningly when Murshid addressed her, and obediently did as Murshid suggested. Murshid said: 'Then we put in the other arm.' — 'And then we close the buttons.' The little girl admiringly looked how Murshid's slender fingers buttoned her jacket.

As it is said in the Arabian legend: 'God brought the soul to ecstasy; then it entered this body of clay.'

Someone told about his perilous adventures when in a small canoe he had followed the course of the Colorado river throught the Grand Canion in Arizona, along places which no human being had ever ventured to cross.

Murshid was asked whether such experiences bring man closer to his soul's realization.

Murshid said: 'It only stimulates his false ego.'

In the multicoloured mountains near the city of Colorado Springs, there is a huge area covered with phantastically shaped gigantic rocks which was considered a place of worship by the American Indians. They had named it 'the Garden of Gods.'

When Murshid arrived there, those who accompanied Him remarked how the clouds which were hanging before and between these strangely fathomed phantoms began to vanish, leaving bare the twisted shapes and grimacing faces.

And it seemed to them as a symbol of what was happening: that the Prophet had come to a garden of gods. The world without a garden of gods: idol-gods of materialism, of commercialism, of competition, of bigotry. The world within a garden of gods: idol-gods of duality, of attachment, of that self which claims: 'I'. And the coming of the Prophet: the clearing away of the clouds of ignorance, the shifting aside of the veils of illusion, which hide behind their folds the idol-gods to which man unknowingly surrenders.

That glance which keeps unwaveringly fixed on the essence of its interest, where was it to be found?

Sometimes the interest was in flowerbeds. And the One Whose own heart is an ever blooming garden, He admired.

Sometimes the interest was in the view on a river, or lake. And One Whose very presence is an ever running stream of beauty, He shared the feelings.

One day the intererest was in an image of Buddha. And the One Who Himself is the living Buddha, He stood before it in loving admiration.

Once Murshid was the guest of a mureed who said: 'This evening, Murshid, I would like to drive you to a place on a rock high above the ocean, from where one sees the sunset as nowhere' else in the world.'

And the One Whose spirit is that Sun which does not know of rising nor of setting, that Sun which always shone and will eternally shine, He smiled.

On one of the last days in New York Murshid visited Kahlil Gilbran, the famous author of 'The Prophet.' He seemed to be so absorbed in the world within his mind, that he was not quite aware of what was going on around him. He asked: 'What has brought you to the Western world, Sir?'

Murshid said: 'A little service.'

Once Murshid was sitting on the deck of the 'Majestic' while sailing from New York to Cherbourg. There were several children running around and shouting so wildly that their number seemed to be hundred although they were only four of five. One of the little boys passed in a run before the chair where Murshid was sitting. He suddenly stopped and became silent and thoughtful. Then, with longing eyes, he asked: 'Are you a King?'

Children are so open to the reality of things.

PART IV

When from the sea* Murshid saw the distant mountains of Italy at sunset, Murshid said: 'It is just like God's golden plate.'

* Adriatic Sea

Murshid once said in connection with someone's recognition of and faith in Rassoul: 'His soul knows, but his mind troubles the vision of his soul.'

On one of the stations between Karachi and Lahore, a young eager looking Hindu-student came to the train-window from where Murshid was looking out. Guided by his soul's inclination, but following only what was known to his mind as highest and greatest in this world, he said: 'Are you Tagore?'

Many strangers always addressed Murshid wherever Murshid went. And the direction of their admirations in life moulded the shape of their questions.

Some simply asked: 'Who are you?' or 'From where do you come?' or they presented their visiting-card, saying: 'May I come and pay you a visit?' When Murshid was wearing the black burnous, many respectfully addressed Murshid as 'Padre', and when Murshid wore the beautiful white muslin clothes, the white anga, the white robe, the white turban, and the white shoes with yellow embroidery, they asked: 'Are you a minister?', 'Of which State are you the minister?' And many only stared, knowing Murshid to be of a caste which one addresses not.

Once a man said to Murshid: 'You must be a rich merchant. What kind of business have you?' Murshid's humble answer has been: 'I am a seller of clothes.'

Many and varied are the garbs of Truth Murshid has given to the world.

Murshid chose His last residence in a place which was a very lonely one.* There were only some cows and goats grazing on the land around the houses. As soon as Murshid came, many Moslim and Hindu families followed, and settled in the surroundings.

Murshid said: 'Wherever the Prophet goes, people will come there.'

(Note: the last words are Murshid's way of saying.)

(* Tilak Lodge, Daya Lane, near Bela Road, Delhi.)

In the mornings Murshid sometimes used to walk up and down the little path at the North-side of the house, in the shadow of the building and of the henna-trees behind it.

Once, while Murshid was walking there, a sage came, with a beggars-bowl in his hand. Murshid addressed him as 'Maharaj.' In answer he greeted   in the way of deepest reverence.

* with joined palms,

The Gujrs are a tribe of professional robbers who live in grass-huts on the other bank of the Jumna. Soon after sunset they begin to burn their fires in the jungle where the jackals howl, and the owls begin to screech in the niem-trees. That is the hour when the past of places becomes more audible, and that sometimes one would rather not go near certain spots.

Murshid said: 'Who is in the protection of Rassoul is always safe.'

Even at times when Murshid seemed to be fully absorbed in the contemplation of other spheres, Murshid saw the slightest demand in the life of those who lived in His surroundings.

Once there was a little boy of the caste for which Murshid has pleaded. He was too old to play with nothing, and not of that evolution which could enable him to do so. With an annoyed expression on his thin little face he was slowly peeling off the bark from a low-bent branch of a henna-tree. When Murshid approached, He softly took out a small silver coin, and covered with it the bare spot on the branch.

The boy did not say anything. He took the coin in his hand and closed his fingers over it and then opened them again.

Then he only looked at Murshid.

Marvellous was the way in which Murshid under all circumstances showed His great patience with and consideration for everybody's needs.

Murshid's servant, Gaffar Ahmed, was a very pious man. He was the happy possessor of a rosary which went four times from one side of the large kitchen-window to the other. Long times during the day it took him to say his prayers, and half the night long the light was burning in his room for their sake.

Murshid once very much wanted Gaffar urgently to take a message to someone in Delhi. After having been told, Gaffar hesitatingly went, and before leaving the room shyly asked: 'Can I do my Nimaz[17] first?'

'Of course', Murshid said, 'after the Nimaz it will be better done.'

By the neighbouring people Murshid was considered to be a great physician and benefactor.

Once a man was brought before Murshid, trembling with fever, and seeming near to the end of his life. Murshid spoke with him, and gave him some innocent little medicine. And a few days later he came with a beaming face: 'You have saved my life.'

Since then many people came to be cured.

Murshid has given to many poor people food and the clothes they so badly needed. And then they came to show themselves in the new garment, uttering words of thankfulness as only an Indian is able to formulate.

Mehtar Chadda said: 'Whenever I will wear this coat, I will remember my Master.'

Murshid was amused on seeing the complete absence of any consideration of time.

There was a tonga-driver[18] who regularly came to fetch Murshid. One day he came an hour before he was told. Murshid said: 'I asked you to come at five, and now it is only four!' He quietly climbed from his carriage and squatted down in the dust of the road, saying: 'Five o'clock will also strike!'

Once he forgot to take his lantern before driving home in the evening, a very punishable fact in Delhi. Seeing the police-man at Kashmiri Gate, he called from far: 'I greet you with folded hands.' The police-man smiled and let him go through.

Murshid one day wanted to settle a business with someone whose address was found with some difficulty. Murshid was brought before a large house in front of which a man was busy shaving himself. Murshid inquired after the proprietor of the house, and received the answer it was that man, shaving there in the street. Murshid sent him a message that Murshid would wish to speak to him. But nothing in the world could affect that man's movements, or take away his attention from his image in the little mirror before him on the wall. He continued his shaving for a long time, and then presented himself before Murshid.

Also the merchants are sitting in their open shops, cross-legged and meditating as if they are concerned about nothing with regard to this earthly plane, neither business nor time. Murshid said: 'Are they not sitting there with the dignity of kings and princes! It seems to be a great favour if one is allowed to come and buy something from them.'

Murshid one day wished to get an article after first seeing about it in different places. After two days Murshid returned to one of the first shops where it was to be had. When Murshid asked for it, (it was something neither subject to fashion, nor liable to a change of any kind) the shop-man mentioned double the price he had wanted for it before. 'But', Murshid said, 'the day before yesterday you offered it for half!' The man was not abashed; not in the least. He quietly said: 'You should have taken it thèn, Sir.'*

Often Murshid spoke about writing a book on India, about the psychology of the people, their philosophical bent of mind, their recklessness, their sense of humour, their

* it was the house: Tilak Lodge

indifference in the good and the bad sense of the word.

Murshid at several occasions said after having been in contact with people: 'In India one finds the best and the worst.'

Once there was a dispute between Mehtar Chadda and his brother-in-law. They both claimed and wanted to be in Murshid's service. They created a great excitement.

Murshid said: 'These simple people have their magic. They can be very powerful. One must never mix in their disputes.'

So Murshid gave the whole affair in the hands of Gaffar, the servant, who was very proud and pleased to have been given that responsibility.

The mehtars are a class of people belonging to the untouchables. Mostly their humble attitude immediately shows who they are considered to be.

Murshid said: 'Their mind is not occupied with so many things. Therefore they can be so powerful.'

Murshid's father once heard a Guru[19] among the mehtars address his chelas.[20] He said: 'In this world we are humbled and trodden upon, but in the next world we shall be kings.'

Murshid said: 'Because they have a crushed ego.'

Murshid once told the example His father had given, when Murshid was a boy, of Indian aristocratic attitude. It concerned the father of Hakim Ajmal Khan whose family is famous far beyond the boundaries of Punjab, and who himself was known for his many cases of miraculous healing.

Murshid's father said: 'No outsider ever saw him laugh.'

Of His mother Murshid one day said: 'She never really laughed, she only smiled.'

Murshid one day spoke of the old Indian doctor's families whose members, generation after generation, cured their patients for the sake of curing them, whose happiness it is to practise their profession for the sake of their profession only.

Murshid said: 'Do you think they accept money for their treatment!'

Murshid said: 'Music in India is now considered as an amusement.' Besides the Qawwals[21] who continue to consider their art to be sacred, there are very few nowadays who see in music something different from a pastime.

Murshid told how in Moula Bakhsh House there used to come two vina-players, famous all over India for their marvellous art. They had the habit of practising all night long. And in order to be kept awake in case they might begin to nod and have a chance of falling asleep, they used to tie their hair with a rope to the ceiling.

Murshid said: 'That is how formerly they acquired their wonderful skill.'

There was a very poor servant who was toiling from morning till evening to provide the sustenance for his family whilst his wife was quietly living, attending to her household duties. If she could have taken some occupation besides, it would certainly have lightened the burden of this man. But he did not wish her to do anything in the way of paid service. So she lived there in their little house and had a comparatively very easy life, while he was slaving all day long.

Murshid said: 'It makes me feel proud of my people.'

In the evening the hunters came back through the ford in the Jumna.[22] They came with a great noice of splashing of their horses, and surrounded by their many pointers which continued their search after game as soon as they reached the shore. Their nose on the ground, they do not leave one inch of land uninvestigated in their eagerness to find some track.

Murshid said: 'They do not smell; they follow their intuition.'

(Note: nowadays scientists say the same)

Murshid once told a story about the kingly attitude of the Maharaja of Baroda.

Someone told the Maharaja: 'There is so much theft in the palace. For instance the carrier of Maharaja-rice, every day he steals from the rice he brings.' (Maharaja-rice is a specially cultivated precious kind of rice with very large grains.) The Maharaja said: 'I will see myself'; and he hid himself in a corner from where he could see everything that was going on. When the rice-carrier had brought in the rice, he carefully looked around to see whether everything was safe; then he took a handful of the rice and put it in his turban. At that moment Maharaja appeared and said: 'Show me what is hidden in your turban!' The trembling man showed the handful of rice. The Maharaja exclaimed: 'You make me ashamed! A thief in the palace should at least become rich.' And he sent for his treasure-keeper and said: 'Give this man pearls of the same size and of the same weight as the rice he has taken.' And turning to the thief he said: 'Now you tell your friends that you have been stealing in the palace!'

This man was rich, as they say in India: 'for many generations to come.'

There lived a woman in Baroda whose mystical powers were so great that she could cause things to happen at her command to an extent which might seem unbelievable to the material-minded.

Once upon a day there came to her a man belonging to a family from which many eminent people had descended. He had several daughters, and ardently wished to have a son. He implored her mystical assistance. And really the long desired son was born. But what never before had occurred in the traditions of that family, this son was blind.

Murshid said: 'It is never wise to try to interfere with the Will of God.'

A little Indian story tells about someone who went to an astrologer to know about his horoscope, and who was told: 'In two days you will die unless you will feed the whole town'. As this was a very poor fellow he was by no means able to accomplish such a thing, and saw his case to be a hopeless one. And so it happened that on the last day of his existence here on earth he sadly wandered out of the town and sat down against the stem of a tree to eat his last scanty meal. When getting up again, he thoughtlessly shook the remaining crumbs of his dinner over an anthill he saw nearby. But to his great surprise the evening fell, and the night passed, and the morning came, and still he felt as alive as before. He sought the astrologer who curiously asked: 'How did you manage it?' This man said: 'Nothing I did, nothing!' The astrologer said: 'It cannot be; tell me what did you do?' Then they found out that by shaking the crumbs of his meal over the nest of the ants he had achieved what was written in the stars: he had fed the whole town.

Murshid said: 'It is their way of teaching love and respect even for the smallest creatures.'

As innumerable as the songs and poems Murshid knew, so manifold were the stories Murshid could tell. And their greatest charm was Murshid's way of telling them. They were not only stories of sages and kings and famous men and women; there was also the tale of the clever boy, and how he got along through life by playing tricks to everyone he met on his way.* One day he became the pupil of a false Teacher. Every morning this Teacher used to seat himself in the midst of his chelas, and to ask them, for the sake of his own glorification, to relate the visions and inspirations they had had during the night. So the Teacher said: 'What happened to you?' And the pupil said: 'O Guru, I saw a shining emerald gate; and when I knocked, it opened by itself. And then I beheld a diamond throne. And on that throne you, Guru, were sitting.' 'Very good,' the Teacher said, 'very good.' 'And what did you see?' he asked another pupil. And the pupil said: 'O Teacher! I heard a celestial song; and when I opened my eyes in a vision I saw angels garbed with light, prostrating themselves to you.' 'That is very good', the Teacher said, 'very good.'

(* the name of this boy was 'You'; this is one of the stories of 'You.')

97

Now it is the custom in India that during the whole night the milk is boiling until in the morning it becomes a delicious kind of cream. And someone has to stir that milk from time to time. So these pupils wanted to have a good long sleep and thought to be very clever in giving their new companion the duty of stirring the milk. But as he had gone without food for some days, he felt very hungry, and could not resist the temptation of tasting a little bit from it. And it felt so comfortable that he tasted until nothing of it remained.

So when it was his turn that the Teacher said: 'And you, what did you see?', he said: 'O Guru, a terrible thing happened! Spirits came, horrible ghosts who made me tremble. And they commanded me to eat from the cream. I resisted. I said: 'I will not do it, I *will* not do it!' But they threatened me. So I had to obey. And they threatened me again and again and again, until it was all finished.'

Murshid said: 'They could not say anything.'

Murshid one day told the story of an Indian queen who was travelling from the palace in one city to the palace in another town. Her carriage was accompanied by horse-guards. After many hours travelling she felt curious about the scenery behind the tight closed curtains of the carriage. She softly shifted them aside. As soon as the horse-guard saw the little hand appear he took his sword and hewed it off.

Afterwards this man was called to justice and was asked how he had been able to do such act. He answered: 'That hand would no more have been of any service to His Majesty.'

Murshid said: 'He was not punished.'

Such a slight little touch is needed for the swing of the pendulam of life to create an immeasurable field of consequences in either the right or the wrong direction. The shadow of a shadow can change all.

The roads across the jungle are borded with trees, the shade of which is more valued there than in any other part of the world.

When these trees are planted they are just a thin little stem with a few leaves. The first days people come to water them; and in order to protect them they plant some cactusses around, just a few. After some time the multiplying leaves of this young tree would attract an army of hungry creatures, but then the cactusses have grown out into a field, surrounding it like an armour. And when the time comes that the branches begin to spread and that their shade becomes a protection against the glaring desert-sun, then the cactusses, which cannot live under a shadow, gradually disappear, of themselves. Then the camels come and eat from the leaves as far as their neck reaches; but nothing can affect the glory of this tree.

Murshid said: 'A picture of freewill and the automatic action of life.'

Before the roads reach their destination, they seem to be lost in a dream. The driver of the carriage dreams, the horse dreams, the land dreams. Nowhere on earth, the dream of life can be realized as on the Indian roads.

One day Murshid wished to attend to the singing of the Qawwāls at a certain appointed time. Murshid addressed the driver who was deeply engaged in the contemplation of eternity. 'I have heard,' Murshid said, 'that this horse runs as fast as a motor-car.' The man seemed to waken to another plane of existence; something opened up in him, and quickened the feelings of this horse.

Never before it has so rapidly arrived at the goal of its journey.

Sometimes it happened while driving back by the road along the Jumna, and on other very dark and lonely places, that a little light was burning at the side of the road, as if a small candle had been placed there in the dust. It was to be seen from far away, and it exerted such attraction that one could hardly draw one's eyes away from it.

Murshid said: 'It may be a magic; better not look at it.'

When the evening-sun weaves its golden veil over the desert, the old road from Delhi to Nizamuddin[23] looks like a vision of another world. It passes through a stretch of land covered with remainings from the time of the olden Mogol dynasties: fortresses, gateways, and other ancient buildings, and many Sufi tombs and Mosques.

At the hours when Murshid saw them, the marble domes seemed so ethereal that they looked as if appearing in a dream.

Murshid said: 'I would I could take one of these beautiful Mosques to the land in Suresnes.'

The tomb of Emperor Humayun is at a few minutes distance from Durgah[24] Hazrat Nizamuddin Aulia. The memorial is situated on an enormous marble platform one reaches after climbing many steps. It dominates a region of hours distance.

Murshid arrived there at sunset while streams of gold were pouring out over the country enhancing the glory of the huge building.

Murshid said: 'It is like a throne on the earth.'

When Emperor Bābar for hundred years had reigned over the land, his son Humayun was struck by an illness which made the end of his life seem near. Then Bābar prayed Allah to let his son live, and to let him die in his place. His prayer was granted. Humayun was restaured to life, and Bābar passed away.

Murshid said: 'He died on his prayer-rug.'

A simple word, when it comes from His lips − it is a living truth.

Murshid much admired the poems of Emperor Zãfar, the Sufi. Notwithstanding their inexpressible sadness, their subtlety is so exquisite that Murshid often used to quote their verses.

When Zãfar was persecuted during the Mutiny, he had taken refuge in the building on Humayun's tomb. And it is there that to visitors the place is shown where he was made a captive. Endless suffering has been caused to him. In the prison his sons were brought, and killed before his eyes. He remained in prison for several years, till the end of his days.

Murshid said: 'He prepared his fate with his own words.'

From the platform of Humayun's memorial tomb one sees next to the building a white and a verdigris dome vaulting over the shrines of the Emperor's barber and of his jeweler.

Murshid said: 'The service of the King made them great.'

There was a sage living in a little shed against a wall which bordered a garden on the bank of the Jumna. He entered it by the one side which was left open. There where it touched the wall it was just high enough that he could sit cross-legged.

Someone remarked: 'How strange to live with not one of the comforts this life can offer.'

Murshid said: 'What is it to a fakir!'

Among the sages one sees the most contradictory types. Some move about in the crowd crying aloud the Name of God; others spend their life in a dark little cell near a saint's tomb. Some cover not only their body, but ever their face with ashes; others make themselves as conspicuous as possible by having coloured ties hanging from their hair.

Murshid said: 'They are all means of crushing the ego to reach annihilation.'

Murshid regurlarly made a walk at the time of the setting sun; sometimes along the footpath on the bank of the Jumna, or along the Bela Road till far beyond Metcalfe House; once to the little Shiva-temple where the stone steps lead to the Jumna below where the Hindus bathe and worship; sometimes to the Kudsia Gardens along the road with the old banyantrees, to the Mosque covered with ivy, in which a little light is burning every night. Murshid always entered by the path at the side, and remained for some time on the open square before the old building. Once Murshid said: 'If I left the world, and went to sit here in silence, thousands would come and be my followers.'

Then came the time of the dark moon in the month of December. Every evening Murshid went along the Bela Road and followed the sandy path that begins near the Mosque with the Sufi's tomb. Then Murshid went through the heavy sand to the Jumna. Darkness comes soon after sunset in India. That is why one could nearly not see the river; one only could hear the soft rippling of its waters. Long times Murshid stood before the black stream. At the other side thousands of jackals were howling in the wilderness. Then Mushid went home in silence.

When Murshid was on the point of returning home after descending the steps which lead from the Jumna Masjid (congregational Mosque) in Delhi, a Madzub[25] came to Murshid. He had strangely concentrated eyes, burning with ecstatic fire. He rushed at Murshid in great joy, saying: 'I have been called to the Court, I have been called to the Court!'

Murshid said: 'I shall soon know what it means.'

It was in the month of December when Murshid wrote the poem which ends with the words: 'Pain is my pleasure; when I laugh then I cry.'

Afterwards, while Murshid was walking on the path along the wall, separating the garden from the jungle, Murshid said: 'The Indian poets, they look for pain.'

(Note: the last words are Murshid's way of saying.)

On December 15th and 16th, 1926 Murshid spoke at the University of Delhi, and on December 22nd, at the Christian College at Lucknow. Murshid was making arrangements to speak at the Moslim University of Aligarh, and intended to give a series of lectures at the Universities of Allahabad, Benares, Hyderabad, Mysore, Madras and Bombay.

Murshid has spoken at Delhi and Lucknow on various aspects of the Sufi Message.

In connection with the subject, Murshid spoke about the existence of the class of untouchables, and with great emphasis has said that the time has come when India should rise above this inhuman institution. Murshid also spoke about the thousands of beggars lying in the streets all over India, and has invoked the spirit of helpfulness of the people of India on their account.

Another point was the intolerance of Hindus and Moslims toward one another. Murshid said: 'The first thing one sees at all the stations is a placard with the inscription 'Hindu water', 'Moslim water.' It is the same water! Why to make that distinction?'

And then Murshid has very much criticized that the people of India could allow their women to be engaged in the making of roads and the building of houses, carrying heavy loads on their heads.

There were many professors and students and distinguished people among Murshid's audience. Murshid said: 'They did not like to hear it, but they all saw that is is true.'

Murshid once said: 'If I took up the work for India, I should have to leave every-thing, everything.'

When Murshid saw the Dilkhusha Palace near Lucknow*, Murshid said: 'If this could be restaured, and become a Sufi Centre!

Murshid for some time has walked up and down in the garden behind the palace.

* which has been dilapidated at the time of the Mutiny,

The population of Lucknow consists for the greatest part of Shias, members of a sect which in name is religious, but originally was political. This sect was created by a leader of the country who did not wish to accept the authority of the Khalif of that time, but wanted to be an independent ruler. His pretext was that on their way to visit that Khalif, the grandsons of Prophet Mohammed, Hassan and Hussain, were killed in a battle for the drinking of the water of a certain well. The Shias are constantly mourning over the death of the grandsons of the Prophet, and use for their rituals, in the places of their sacred meetings, an imitation of the tombs of Hassan and Hussain.

Seeing the harsh expression on the face of the majority of the Shias, Murshid said: 'It is because they keep before their mind a tomb, instead of the living Word of the Prophet.'

At Tenfields Garden* Murshid remained for a long time listening to the twittering of many little birds, those miniature Indian birds which are coloured with a thousand shining colours.

Murshid said: 'They are like living jewels.'

(*near Lucknow.)

A guide accompanied Murshid in the compound of the Golden Temple in Benares. Like all those who saw Murshid, he was keenly interested. At the moment of Murshid's leaving he asked: 'What caste is yours?'

Murshid answered by quoting the verse of Kabir[26]: 'Santan jat na pucho nirguniyan', 'Ask not the worshipper of God the caste to which he belongs...'

At the moment Swami Shradanand was killed at Delhi by a fanatic Moslim, Murshid had an accident at Benares. Murshid was much hurt while getting out of a carriage. Murshid was extremely sad about the murder of the Swami, whom Murshid had visited a few days before, as it was a new stumbling block on the path to the unity of the two religions, Hinduism and Islam.

The same afternoon town-criers proclaimed in all the prominent cities of India that the Hindu-shops had to be closed, and a great propaganda started at once among Hindus, for the new martyr Shradanand.

Afterwards Murshid said: 'This accident was the reaction of the murder, on Rassoul.'

(The Swami was shot on Dec. 25th 1926, in his own room.)

Near one of the burning ghats[27] on the bank of the Ganges at Benares there is a little house where it is said that in olden times King Haris Chandra collected the fees from those who came to have their dead cremated.

Murshid told the story of King Haris Chandra. That one day the Rishis were conversing, and they have wondered whether there existed on earth one human being who was fully dependable. And the answer was: 'One there is. His name is King Haris Chandra! But they said: 'King Haris Chandra! He has got all that the heart could wish. He has a prospering kingdom; his subjects adore him; he has a loving wife, and a promising son. How can we know whether he is really dependable?' Then the Rishis have agreed to test King Haris Chandra. One of them has gone in the guise of a sage, saying: 'King Haris Chandra, will you grant me a wish?' And King Haris Chandra, who was at the service of sages, said: 'Yes, I will grant it.' The Rishi said: 'King Haris Chandra, I would wish to be king over this country.' And Haris Chandra went to his wife and said: 'Come with me, I am no longer King.' And they have gone, he and his wife and their little son, on foot to the neighbouring country. And when they had reached the boundary, the Rishi has appeared, saying: 'You have travelled so many days in my kingdom, now pay me the tax you owe me.' Haris Chandra said: 'Nothing I have with which I can pay you.' But the Rishi said: 'Haris Chandra, you gave me your word that I am the king of this land, so pay me the tax.' Then Haris Chandra has sold his wife and his son as slaves to be able to pay the tax to the king of the country. And he himself has entered into the service of the one who owned the burning ghat at Benares, and at the entrance has collected the money for his master. – While he was doing that work his little son fell suddenly ill, and died. And his wife came with her dead boy in her arms, that he might be cremated at the burning ghat. Haris Chandra put forward his hand to receive her due. But what has a poor slave to offer? She had nothing to give. Then Haris Chandra kept faithful to his master, and refused her to enter.

At that moment the Rishi has put an end to the test. He has restored the dead prince to life, and made Haris Chandra again King over his country.

This is the legend which is known all over India in the form of a drama, and which fascinated Murshid when Murshid was a boy. He used to play it with His comrades; that is to say, He stood behind them, He spoke the words they had to utter and made their hands perform the movements which were required.

But who acted was He alone.

From sunrise till sunset the water-carriers go over the roads with their walk as gracious and flexible as the movements of the stick over their shoulder on which hang the gleaming copper pots filled with the sacred water of the Jumna.

It is said in India that Ganges and Jumna come from one spring in Himalaya. In the valley they divide, and then come again together, showing thereby the picture of life: the primal oneness of God and soul; the seeming separation in the mortal existence; and the reunion in God again. By worshipping both rivers, the Hindus worship the immanence of God in the ever − running stream of life; and thus their worship, although offered to the river with rituals and flowers and other symbols, in reality is Truth-worship.

When the Maharaja of Jaipur went to Europe, he took with him tanks full of the water of the Ganges.

Murshid said: 'India is a land of ideal.'

When Murshid saw the lace-work of marble at Emperor Akbar's memorial tomb at Sikandra*, Murshid said: 'It is like India's music. They have made music out of a stone.'

(* there where once the Koh-i-Noor has been kept.)

There is an extraordinary resonance in the dome of Taj Mahal[28]. Every sound becomes a song when uttered there where is Noor Jahan's* memorial tomb.

When Murshid entered, many people were loudly speaking, and someone was demonstrating, by singing single notes, how long the music of the voice continues before it dies away in vibrations which become softer and softer until they extinguish in a far away distance. Here one knows that no sound ever really ceases, but for always continues in planes beyond human perception. The mingling of the many differen voices made a symphony of inexpressible beauty. It lifted one to the spheres where angels sing the glory of God for ever and ever and for eternity.

Murshid stood for a long time in the corner at the right side of the entrance, silent.

*Murshid always used to call Taj Bibi: 'Noor Jahan', 'The Light of the World'.

While listening to the music in the dome of Taj Mahal, Murshid looked at the structure of the building ad said: 'This art has been lost now.'

From the platform, near the marble tank, Murshid looked back at Taj Mahal. Murshid began a sentence: 'It makes me sad to think...' Murshid did not continue. After a little while Murshid said: 'These people knew what grandeur is.'

On seeing the Moti Masjid in the Fort at Agra, Murshid said: 'Imagine! This is standing here unused, and hardly anyone looks at it!'

(Moti Masjid means Pearl Mosque.)

On several stations of the side-line from Delhi to Baroda there are troops of Hanuman-monkeys, different kind than one sees in the North. They have long tails, black faces, and black hands and feet. They come and sit in the windows of the train-compartments, and stretch out their hands, eager to get fruit or sweets from the passing travellers.

Murshid never for one moment allowed them to remain sitting there.

When going to Khwaja Moinuddin Chishti's tomb[29] Murshid always took a parcel with food for the poor. Although there were many poor people on the way through the different archgates to the square near Khwaja's durgah, where the Qawwals were singing their songs of praise, Murshid sometimes kept this parcel with Him for a long time.

Murshid said: 'Someone must ask for food.'

One day there was the need of a fire, and there was nothing to start it with. There were only many letters, all of which had been answered.

Murshid said: 'Never burn any letters; always tear them with a wish, connected with the action of tearing: 'May difficulties be scattered', or: 'May clouds be dispersed', anything suited to the circumstances.'

At all the tombs of Sufis and emperors and kings, a race of guardians has sprung from the children of the first guardians, and the children of their children, and so on. Thus it has happened that on Khwaja Moinuddin Chishti's tomb at Ajmer two thousand guardians are divided over the many different activities in connection with the saint's tomb. But this guardianship mostly degenerates into a money-making-business. When visitors arrive, an army of sweepers begins to sweep the imaginary dust from marble walls which are purity itself; others spend their life in collecting money near some transparent spot of the marble, or near some curiosity they have fashioned themselves. Everything worth visiting is commercialised to a degree one can hardly imagine.

Murshid said, after visiting the tomb of Khwaja Moinuddin Chishti at the time of the Urs:[30] 'There are many people who have become so disgusted by it that they nevermore visit the tombs of the saints. But what is it after all! Only something to be overlooked in order to see what really is there: the living example.'

Often and often Murshid was moved to tears on hearing the songs of the Qawwäls on the tombs of the Sufi saints.

One day Murshid said: 'What touched me most was the verse he sang: 'All inspiration comes from here'.'

Murshid one day told the story of a mureed who was drowning in a river. The water of the river was coming over his head. He called loudly in his distress: 'Murshid, Murshid, I am drowning!' And a hand appeared to save him. But before taking it he asked: 'Murshid?' And a voice said: 'No, a friend.' He did not take that hand. Again he called: 'Murshid, Murshid!'. And a hand appeared. He asked: 'Murshid?' And a voice said: 'No, God.' He did not take that hand. With his last efforts he called: 'Murshid, O Murshid!' And there care a hand to his rescue. He asked: 'Murshid?' And a voice said: 'Yes, Murshid.' This hand he took.

And he was saved.

Some time before He entered the Kingdom of His glory Murshid told about a certain Murshid, who was asked by his mureeds to explain to them a verse on annihilation. All the Murshid answered was: 'One day I will show you.' So one day when that verse was sung, the Murshid passed away.

Murshid Himself gave the example of what He has taught us: to rise above the difficulties and jarring influences of daily life. Even in the midst of suffering Murshid has still seen the funny side of things.

Gaffar Ahmed had a great difficulty in speaking; he did not clearly pronounce words and stammered very much.

During the illness, on one of the last days of His personal presence among us, Murshid said: 'Now I see the advantage of being a Maharaja. When he is ill, his Court-musicians come and play before him, so that he can forget his pain.' Then Murshid smiled and said: 'Would you not ask Gaffar to come and sing for me?'

Murshid had often warned for the use of the ideal: 'Without differences and distinctions', leading to what Murshid called: 'universal ideas'. Not knowing, or forgetting, that 'the God-Ideal'* is the bridge connecting the limited life with the unlimited', and that 'whoever travels over this bridge passes safely from the limited to the unlimited life', the traveller on the Path is apt to lose the track on following these universal ideas about the Message and the Messenger.

Veiling a reminder of truth behind a humorous simile, Murshid said, at an occasion when for a distinct purpose, a cloth had to be used, seemingly similar to several others: 'Is it the universal cloth?'

* (The 'God-Ideal' as understood by the mureeds.)

A few days before Murshid went to the other side of life, Murshid said, looking at Gayan and Vadan lying next to the bed: 'They are the Koran of the present time.'

In those last days Murshid sometimes wished to hear the reading of the sayings of Vadan. On hearing the words: 'Waves, why does the wind come and then go from you?' 'It comes to wake us, and leaves us to solve the problem among ourselves', Murshid said: 'The Messenger.'

One of those moments when His soul was loosening its hold on that garb which for some time gave us the impression that He was closer to us than He always is, and always will be, Murshid said: 'When the unreality of life pushes against my heart, its door opens to the reality.'

At another time Murshid said: 'If you are annoyed by any disagreeable experience, it is a loss; but if you have learnt by it, it is a gain.'

Always, till the very end, Murshid has remained without any outward sign of illness.

Murshid Himself saw it on one of the last days. Murshid said: 'It is prophetic.'

Murshid passed away in the South-room of Tilak Lodge, Daya Lane, near Bela Road Delhi, on Saturday, Febr. 5th 1927, at 8.20 in the morning. Murshid left no indication whatsoever, neither about people nor about place.

The Scriptures speak of earthquakes having taken place at the time when the Lord Buddha had passed, also after Jesus Christ had been crucified. It seems to be a symbolical representation of what happened after Their passing in the hearts and lives of their disciples, of its effect upon the work They left behind, and upon the world in general.

In the evening, following the passing of Murshid, a tremendous thunderstorm made the houses tremble. From all sides of the horizon lightnings came, and flashed without ceasing for a long, long time.

Murshid one day spoke the words, the liberating words, which lead the soul to its home-land, which lift it far beyond the fleeting shadow-play of life, here and in the hereafter.

Murshid said: 'Look at Me.'

Verily, the soul of Rassoul is the Light of the universe.

Glossary

Page 13- 1 Murshid = Master, teacher. The title with which Murshid Inayat Khan was addressed by his disciples.

Page 15- 2 Maula Baksh = Murshid Inayat Khan's maternal grandfather, a famous musician.

Page 16- 3 Nabi = Prophet of God; bringer of God's Message.

Page 23- 4 Mureed = disciple.

Page 26- 5 Fazal Manzil = Blessed dwelling-place; the house in Suresnes where Murshid Inayat Khan lived from 1922-1926.

Page 26- 6 Viladat Day = 5th July. Murshid Inayat Khan's birthday.

Page 28- 7 Abbá = Father.

Page 28- 8 Mamuli = Khair-un-nisa or Claire; Murshid Inayat Khan's younger daughter.

Page 30- 9 Bhaijan = Pirzade Vilayat Inayat Khan, Murshid Inayat Khan's eldest son.

Page 31-10 Bhaiyajan = Murshidzade Hidayat Inayat Khan, Murshid Inayat Khan's younger son.

Page 33-11 Oriental room = the room in Fazal Manzil where Murshid Inayat Khan gave interviews.

Page 39-12 The Message = the Sufi Message.

Page 50-13 Maya = illusion.

Page 50-14 Rassoul = Prophet of God, Who has delivered His Message.

147

Page 60-15   Kabbala = Jewish mystical book.
Page 61-16   Burrak = legendary horse, which carried the Prophet Mohammed to Jerusalem and to the heavenly spheres.
Page 82-17   Nimaz = prayer.
Page 84-18   Tonga = little cart with two wheels drawn by a horse.
Page 88-19   Guru = teacher.
Page 88-20   Chela = disciple.
Page 91-21   Qawwals = musicians who sing and play at the shrines of the holy men.
Page 93-22   Jumna = one of the holy rivers of India.
Page 103-23   Nizamuddin = village outside Delhi, where the great Sufi saint Nizamuddin Aulia lies buried.
Page 104-24   Durgah = the tomb of a saint.
Page 111-25   Madzub = dervish immersed in God.
Page 119-26   Kabir = great mystical poet of India, admired by Hindus and Moslims alike.
Page 121-27   Ghats = steps leading to the river.
Page 126-28   Taj Mahal = the beautiful mausoleum built at Agra by Emperor Shah Jehan for his wife Noor Jehan.
Page 131-29   Khaja Moinuddin Chisti = great Sufi saint buried at Ajmer (Rajasthan).
Page 133-30   Urs = anniversary of death.

148